Selling with EASE

The Ultimate Field Sales Handbook

VARDA KREUZ

Selling with EASE

The Ultimate Field Sales Handbook

2nd Edition

The ultimate field sales resource, breaking the sales process down into four, easy to understand stages;
Earn the right; Ask the appropriate questions; Solve the problem & Execute the solution.

Chris Murray

Publisher's note
Every possible effort has been made to ensure that the information contained in this book is accurate at the time of going to press, and the publishers and author cannot accept any responsibility for any errors or omissions, however caused. No responsibility for loss or damage occasioned to any person acting, or refraining from action, as a result of the material in this publication can be accepted by the editor, the publisher or the author.

First published in 2010
Second edition 2011

Apart from any fair dealing for the purpose of research or private study, or criticism or review, as permitted under the Copyright, Designs and Patents Act 1988, this publication may only be reproduced, stored or transmitted, in any form or by any means, with the prior permission in writing of the publishers, or in the case of reprographic reproduction in accordance with the terms and licences issued by the CLA. Enquiries concerning reproduction outside these terms should be sent to the publishers at the under mentioned address:

VARDA KREUZ LIMITED
82 King Street
Manchester M2 4WQ
United Kingdom

Tel: +44 (0)161 935 8183
www.vardakreuztraining.com

© Chris Murray 2010, 2011

The right of Chris Murray to be identified as author of this work has been asserted by him in accordance with the Copyright, Designs and Patents Act 1988.

ISBN 9781849140799

First published in Great Britain in 2010

Praise from Readers for *Selling with EASE – The Ultimate Field Sales Handbook*

"This is a great read and simple format for any sales team to follow. It doesn't matter what or where you are selling…the same rules apply!"
- *Leonard Patterson Area Sales Director USA*

"Thanks very much for the ultimate field sales book, excellent tips and some great info. I'll certainly have you on my list when I next look for sales training."
- *Phil Keenan Director UK*

"Simply great work. Very useful."
- *Sharad Dua Human Resources India*

"Great book - well written and full of really useful nuggets."
- *Phil Broughton Head of Sales UK*

"Thanks; wonderful. We need Varda Kreuz in India."
- *Anup Soans Author & Program Director India*

"Thank you, this is extremely helpful."
- *Mustafa Awwad Sales Manager Kuwait*

"This is wonderful!"
- *Laurie Shafer Account Manager USA*

"I have had many salespersons call on me over the years who could benefit greatly from this book."
- *Ewan Ogilvie Director UK*

"Amazing job… great book!"
- *Marcio Miranda Account Executive Brazil*

"Thanks Chris for your great book, very useful."
- *Koen Vanderhoydonk Client Relationship Management Belgium*

"I just love this handbook! Thank you"
- *Verna Z. Waite Independent Insurance Sales Person USA*

"Chris, this is simply written, with good content and well laid out. Good stuff!"
- *Haydn Wall International Sales Manager Australia*

"Your book is fantastic - very well laid out and easy to read, congratulations!"
- *Neil Aremband Managing Director UK*

"EXCELLENT!!"
- *Valeria Morado Spain*

"This is exactly what I was needed. I find your book an excellent tool for our sales team in addition to the other sales techniques and training tools we have."
- *Slavdo Todorov General Manager Bulgaria*

Contents

Foreword

Introduction

Part 1: Before We Start

Why We Are Here	15
Selling With EASE - The Fundamentals	17
o **E**arn the Right	18
o **A**sk the Appropriate Questions	18
o **S**olve the Problem	18
o **E**xecute the Solution	19
Appearance	20
First Impressions	21
Selling Tools	22
Attitude	25

Part 2: Planning and Preparation

What We Need To Do and Why We Need To Do It	28
Journey Plans	29
Do You Deliver Value or Cost?	31
Key Times to Plan and Prepare	33
Setting Objectives	37
o Types of Objective	37
o SMART Objective Setting	39

Part 3: Selling With EASE - Earn the Right

Coffee Break Catch Up Number 1	46
Outlet Check	48
Building Rapport	49
Coffee Break Catch Up Number 2	51
Deep Listening	54

Part 4: Selling With EASE - Ask the Appropriate Questions

Questioning Techniques	57
o Types of Questions	58
o Misconceptions About Questioning Techniques	60
Coffee Break Catch Up Number 3	62

Part 5: Selling With EASE – Solve the Problem

Features, Advantages & Benefits	67
o So, What Are Features?	70
o So, What Are Benefits	71
Coffee Break Catch Up Number 4	72

Part 6: Selling With EASE - Execute the Solution

The Presentation	75
o Sales Presenter	75
o Samples	77
o POS	77
Closing	78
o Buying Signals	79
o Types of Close	80
Handling Objections	82
o Justified or Unjustified?	84
o Anticipating Objections	85
o Special Situation Objections	86
Fear of Price	91

Part 7: Administration and Post Call Evaluation

Sales Figures	95
Customer Records	96
Evaluation	99

Foreword

When I was a Sales Director looking for sales trainers to improve my team – to give them the great start that I'd had within larger organisations - I wanted someone that completely understood the role of a field sales team and the market in which I operated.

I didn't find them!

One of the main reasons I formed Varda Kreuz Training and the On Trade Sales Academy stemmed from those frustrations and they were reflected in my reasoning for writing this handbook – there simply isn't enough out there to help field sales people, especially not for the FMCG* side of things.

Sure there's lots of generic work, but nothing for someone stumbling into their first field sales job or looking for a useful refresher.

If you have any questions, feel free to contact me on the office line - +44 (0) 161 935 8183 - if I'm around I'll take the call, if I'm training one of our delightful reception staff will take your details and I'll call you back as soon as I'm free.

You can also e-mail me (ultimatefieldsales@vardakreuztraining.com) with any suggestions for the third edition, your thoughts on this one or just for a general chat regarding field sales team training – either way I'd love to hear from you.

I hope you enjoy reading the book as much as I did writing it.

Best regards,

Chris Murray

*FMCG – Fast Moving Consumer Goods

Introduction

Throughout the book there are a series of icons, features and signposts to help you find some of the ideas in the book quickly just when you need them

 **Put Yourself in Their Shoes** – This is just about the best way to figure out what the customer is after

 **Quick Fix** – A few ideas to get you back on track

 You Decide – Not everything is black and white, sometimes your own personality and judgement have to come into play.

 True Story – Only the names have been changed to protect the innocent (and a few friends!)

 **Time Out** – A short reflection or summary with reference to the current topic

1

Before We Start

90% of your competition are – at best – extremely average!

As a collective, they have received very little (if any) training.
Most of the really good ones have been promoted to management positions, most of the really poor ones have been floating round for years.

> **By the way, always be wary of someone who says they have twenty years experience in the same job, that isn't twenty years experience; it's the same year twenty times.**

Of the remaining 10%, only two out of each ten are exceptional and the other eight do an alright job; they are the pleasant dependable ones who make the difference on a daily basis.

So if all the above is true - and I admit on reading it for the first time, it sounds a little harsh – this job should be a doddle, shouldn't it?

Well yes and no.

First of all - well done you for starting to read this!

You are willing to give up your own time for a little self-improvement, which is one of the things which will set you apart from the other 90%.

If you are willing to become better tomorrow than you were today, then your future is already in better shape than most.

Secondly, just being better than the competition isn't enough (remember they aren't that good to begin with), I'm afraid you have customers to contend with too – and they are the real reason someone trusted you with those fancy business cards and that boot full of samples.

So, throughout this handbook we'll discuss how to deal with customers, how the top 10% of the profession do what they do and fill the rest of the pages with stuff that has helped me out many times in the past.

There is nothing in here that is simply based on theory.

If it wouldn't sound or look right standing in front of a customer, you will not read it in these pages.

So to start us off, think about this - you're busy, two members of staff haven't turned up, three important items were missing off your delivery, the sales are down year on year - and all of a sudden some upstart in a bad suit walks in and starts talking about a sport you don't care about and the traffic they've just been stuck in!

Why We Are Here

This may sound a little obvious, but first of all you must understand this – YOU ARE IN SALES.

It was on the job advert you applied for, it is the purpose of the department you work in, and it might even be in your title.

The rest of your company is depending on you to bring home the business that keeps them all in a job.

If you are reading this because you hope to get into sales, then that statement probably doesn't worry you too much, I'm sure you are desperate to rise to the challenge.

And yet when some people put on the sales hat and walk into an outlet to sell, they completely forget their purpose within their company.

There can be nothing more annoying than sales people walking into your business who don't know why they are there.

If you are a polite, easy going customer you let them finish and then ask them to leave, if you are not polite – well, they just don't get a chance to start.

Figure 1 gives some indication to why we are there, pretending we have just 'nipped in' isn't fooling anyone – you are either there to help, become a customer yourself or get in the way. Which one do you think?

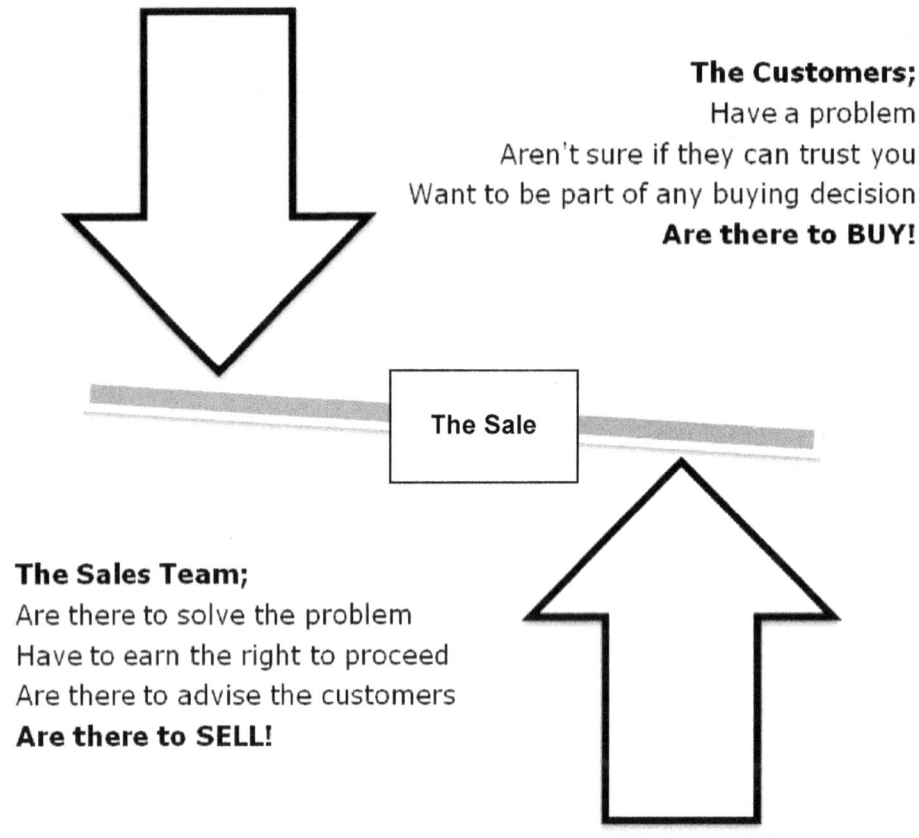

Figure 1 - Understanding the Customer / Salesperson Relationship

Selling with EASE - The Fundamentals

Throughout this handbook we will be following the Varda Kreuz Selling with EASE System.

As shown in Fig 2, this follows four steps

1. **E**arn the right
2. **A**sk the appropriate questions
3. **S**olve the problem
4. **E**xecute the solution

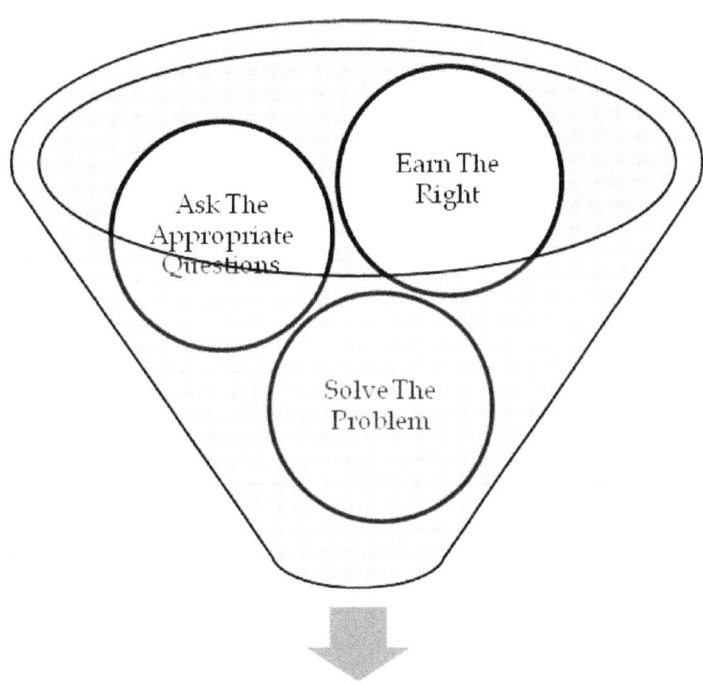

Figure 2 - Selling with EASE

Earn the right

We will talk about presenting ourselves in a professional manner, how we approach the sales situation and why customers decide to go with your recommendation.

Ask the appropriate questions

Being able to understand a situation well enough to present a solution needs a particular set of questioning skills and the equally important ability to listen to the answers.

Solve the problem

When we fully understand the situation, when we know what it is that we have within our toolbox which will deliver a benefit to the customer we present it professionally and effectively.

Remember this; when a customer walks into a DIY store to buy a drill, he doesn't really want a drill – he wants a hole!

A bad salesperson will present all the drills that are on offer, a good salesperson will discuss the desired hole with the customer.

Your products deliver benefits and solve problems for customers; do you know what they are?

Execute the solution

Once you have solved the problem, you put that solution into action.

That means knowing how to ask for the sale (or close), follow through with the required administration and keeping all your promises to the customer and your employer.

It is up to you to make sure everything that should happen does happen. Don't blame other departments, other people will let you down – fact; but as a sales department we cannot let our customers down.

> *"Life is often compared to a marathon, but I think it is more like being a sprinter; long stretches of hard work punctuated by brief moments in which we are given the opportunity to perform at our best."*
> – **Michael Johnson**

Appearance

So now we have established that everyone expects sales people to sell and we have an outline of how we are going to go about it, we move on to making sure that people want to speak to us when we enter their domain.

真 When I was an account manager I had a colleague who missed out on promotion because the Sales Director referred to him as looking like "an unmade bed" (ouch).

Later on in my career when I was trying to convince anyone who would listen how important appearance is to the sales process, I was given a line by an incredibly well dressed member of the team and that line was *"You just never know who you might meet!"*

And he was right, you just don't know if you will walk into an outlet and find that the competition are in there (embarrassing), or the Head of Sales from another company who is about to interview you for that career changing job next week (career threatening), or the buyer of the biggest retail chain in the country (when you do finally get promoted, trust me, they'll remember) or maybe the person your boss reports to will just shows up to see how you are getting on.

> *"Everything that irritates us about others can lead us to an understanding of ourselves"*
> - **Carl Gustav Jung**

First Impressions

Allegedly you have the time it takes for a short match to burn itself out to make a first impression.

In ninety seconds they are 90% sure of whether they will give you the time of day, stop what they are currently doing or whether they think they will like you or not.

My best advice is this; Dress appropriately for the situation you are in!

Be slightly more formal than the person you are meeting – not over dressed or over casual – dress appropriately.

Ensure that what you are wearing is presentable, clean and pressed.

Ensure that your personal appearance is acceptable (you know what I mean – hair, hands, face) and that whatever you ate or drank last night is camouflaged with something minty.

I'm sure that you have been served by someone before now who looked like 'an unmade bed', whose personal odour was a mixture of BO, garlic and nicotine, and then pointed something out with dirty nails.

It is horrible being served by someone with only one of these traits; make sure it is not you.

Selling Tools

When you started on your first day, there was probably someone very pleasant who handed you a selection of selling tools. These would have consisted of pens, business cards, presenters, product samples, sample POS (Point of Sale – marketing materials to be used at the **P**oint **O**f **S**ale), customer record sheets, planning documents and A4 brand talkers.

If you didn't get all these don't worry, not everyone does, you may have received many more useful bits and bobs which you stored neatly in your new plastic storage box in the boot of your new car – well done you.

Two months later you are asking the customer if they have a pen you can borrow, promising to drop things off on your 'next' visit because you have 'just given away the last one' and generally hoarding things in places around your house that you have never used but 'looked useful' when you were in head office.

I do not know what you need to fulfil every part of your job, but I do know that you should have it – whatever it is - ready for whenever it is required.

- ✓ Do not leave the house without more than two working pens and some business cards.
- ✓ Look at where you are going that day and pack the appropriate samples and POS.
- ✓ Set yourself some objectives and pack the presentation tools required to achieve them.
- ✓ However you keep your customer records or reports, keep them up to date throughout the day if you can.

If your business doesn't create a selling tools pack for you, create one yourself

Imagine this, you run a business, the sales person has dazzled you with their professional appearance and attitude, then just as you are about to shake their hand and thank them for the solution to your problem, they say;

"I wasn't really ready for this; I'm back around here again in about six weeks! See you then"

In reality, what happens most of the time is this:

- Salesperson wasn't ready for anything – selling something was a complete surprise
- Salesperson promises customer the world
- Salesperson calls overworked department in head office
- Salesperson gives them a sob story about how the sale will be lost if the customer doesn't go top of the pile

The trouble is every department, in every head office get these calls every day – and while most are incredibly accommodating – the sales team never stand back and realise how selfish they are being, making the rest of their office based colleagues work twice as hard as they should be.

> *"When you do more than what you are paid for, you will soon be paid more for what you do."*
> — **Zig Ziglar**

真 The Chief Accountant at a major Whisky business had this sign above his desk;

Do not make your lack of preparation my emergency

It didn't matter if you ran into his basement office with the most important proposal the company had ever seen, he believed everyone could plan their time effectively, and he demanded the respect to be allowed to plan his time effectively too.

So get yourself ready to sell, prepare the tools you need in advance, because (if you remember) selling is what we are here for!

Attitude

 There is an old Victorian sales story.....

This involves two shoe salesmen who visit deepest darkest Africa for the very first time.

Both are from rival companies and both are highly regarded for their ability as the respective best salesperson within their ranks.
As they find their first group of indigenous Africans, it becomes clear that no one in the tribe wears shoes.

Both men hurry back to London to relay the news to their respective employers, the first one walks into the board room and announces,

'There is no business to be had in deepest, darkest Africa; nobody wears shoes!'

The second chap bursts into his offices and shouts,

'Quick, we need to build a factory in deepest, darkest Africa; nobody wears shoes yet!'

Now, as my old boss used to say "You have got to fish where the fish are", but remember this - the attitude you get up with in the morning is the attitude you are going to be stuck with.

Don't chase impossible rainbows, do be aware of your opportunities, make sure you are ready for them to surface and grab them.

Nobody likes to deal with a miserable, moaning, woe is me type.

As Barnabas Kreuz points out "No one ever kicked a dog wagging its tail my boy, no one ever kicked a dog wagging its tail."

2

Planning and Preparation

"Obstacles are things a person sees when he takes his eyes off his goal."
E. Joseph Cossman

Planning and preparation is enough to fill most sales people with dread.

There are some who seem to think of themselves akin to wild stallions, unbridled, free.

Any attempt to harness the raw power of their sales brilliance, would only diminish its blinding light – practise would smother the genius of their irresistible improvisation.

Well for all those out there who feel that way; I'm afraid it's time to rub your eyes and have an honest look at the real world.

Every now and again you might pull off a 'doozy' – you may have thought the customer was overwhelmed by your quick wittedness and *savoir faire* - but on the whole people will think you are unreliable and unprepared!

So stop being envious about the sales people who seem to glide in, looking and sounding great and walk out with the order, it wasn't luck – they plan, prepare and practise.

What We Need to Do and Why We Need to Do It

Planning our calls is crucial; however I am fully aware of the percentage of sales people out there just getting up, getting dressed, jumping in a car and ending up somewhere – it didn't really matter where.

Planning properly means that we;

- Look professional
- Are more likely to meet our planned objectives
- Have an inner feeling of security, knowing what you are supposed to be doing.

In turn this will give you greater results, which will increase your job satisfaction and help to reduce stress to a far more bearable level.

Being in control of each and every call through proper preparation will even generate results for the inexperienced amongst you, remember 90% of your competition are absolutely hopeless; being this much better cannot do you any harm.

We have got to decide where we are going to go, what we want to achieve when we get there and how we will achieve that outcome.

Remember, we are only going where the business is, so we don't want to waste too much time in calls that won't bear fruit.

With that in mind, let's decide where we are going to.

Journey Plans

If your company has a system in place already that's fine, just make sure that your long term journey plan allows you to;

- ✓ Be in specific sectors of your region on different days of the week throughout the month
- ✓ Be flexible for emergencies
- ✓ Hit your targets.

When I ran a national field sales team there was constant conversation regarding sales people being called to the same area of their patch over and over, while other parts of the sales region were being totally neglected.

真 One day when a member of the field sales team was ill, an irate and extremely angry customer called from a remote part of the country demanding immediate action. The only way I could appease him was by travelling to his premises, at that moment, to find a solution.

Once up there I solved the problem, settled the customer down and we began to talk about how he was treated by the ill team member and his other suppliers.

He told me, with a smile on his face, about a company that were chasing him for his business, however the representative was only ever in his town once a month on a Monday – and there was never anybody in on a Monday, they were closed.

The representative knew this, but that was the only time he was in the area, Monday was his day to be there, nothing could change it.

So every Tuesday, the owner would open his door and find a business card pushed through the door to prove that he had been *'visited'* by the salesman.

I'm willing to wager that every time the card went through the door, it went on the salespersons weekly report as a call as well.

Waste of time, waste of petrol and a waste of business cards.

 ## The Six Day Journey Plan

Divide your region / sales patch into six areas based on the size of the opportunity or number of customers.
i.e. If a region has an abundance of customers or prospects, then split that into two or three of the areas, just make sure that each of the six is equal in business and opportunity not square miles.

Now, place them into your diary like so

Monday	Tuesday	Wednesday	Thursday	Friday
Area 1	Area 2	Area 3	Area 4	Area 5
Area 6	**Area 1**	Area 2	Area 3	Area 4
Area 5	Area 6	**Area 1**	Area 2	Area 3
Area 4	Area 5	Area 6	**Area 1**	Area 2

In this example, at the start of the next month, the sales person would be in Area 3 on the first Monday

As you can see, with this simple method you are in a different part of your territory, everyday, across a month.

If a customer asks to see you, you are aware of when you will next be in the neighbourhood and can suggest the next two opportunities for a call, if there is an emergency away from where you should be, you can ensure that your normal work can be in a pivotal corner of the area to cut down on travel time and expense.

Do You Deliver Value or Cost?

We should be aiming to become professional, effective and efficient. It doesn't bother most sales people how much they cost their business, taking for granted that they are somehow *'owed the job'*.

Every time you walk through the door into a customer's premises you cost your company money.

 Try this exercise:

£   Add up your annual salary, the expenses you claim over a year and a third of the original cost of your company car.

÷ 40   Got a figure? Right - divide it by forty.

÷ ?   Now take that and divide it by the number of **meaningful** calls (no, really – the real number) you actually do per week.

=   That is how much it costs to put you through every door you visit, whether you come out with a result or not.

Q   So if it was your business, would you pay someone else that much money to walk through a customer's door and come out with nothing, if they made no difference what so ever?

Here's an idea;

How about you give your company half that much every time you go on a call and they give it you back if you bring out five times that much **IN PROFIT**!

Do you see how important it is to focus your efforts on real potential customers?

If your call doesn't equate to a 60% chance of becoming a future, genuine buying customer, you probably have better things to do.

Don't get me wrong, it might not be until the twentieth call or the fifth conversation – but the call has to be going somewhere, it has to have potential and it has to end up being profitable.

But even those odds mean nothing if you don't personally perform, would you buy off someone who didn't deliver and match up to your expectations?

Therefore, thoroughly planning your day, your call cycle and what you intend to talk about in each call is paramount.

Remember, the natural, lucky salesperson isn't lucky – he or she creates their own luck, makes themselves successful.

Chance, winging it, letting things take their natural course – these are things that failures do and then blame their eventual downfall on everything, and everybody, else.

> *"The gods help them that help themselves."*
> – **Aesop**

Key Times to Plan and Prepare

Sales Meetings

A well run sales meeting should give you the opportunity to rephrase what you do for a living into what the business expects you to achieve.

The Night Before

Give yourself enough time at the end of each working day to prepare for the next one.

I won't think you're a hero for working a twelve hour day, settling down for two hours of admin and then planning tomorrow way into the early hours of the morning.

Just work your planning process into your day, but make it the day before, not just before you leave the house half dressed with a piece of toast in your mouth.

Make sure you have covered the basics for an easy, stress free start to the day.

- Journey plan
- Relevant equipment and sales tools
- Samples
- A clean and roadworthy car.

Then for each pre-planned call, make sure you have;

- ✓ A clear objective (what can't you leave the call without achieving? It doesn't have to be a sale every time, it might be a second appointment, or a promise of a trial – just set a target)
- ✓ What happened last time you called
- ✓ Customer information
- ✓ Promotional activity presentation or POS material
- ✓ Your sales presentation

Before each call

Just before you go in have a quick look over your;

- Objectives
- Call history
- Sales tools and equipment
- Presentation
- Personal appearance – would you buy from you?

After the call

While you are still flushed with a post-call glow, make sure you;

- Review your performance versus your objectives
- Make a list of follow up actions and required admin
- Put in place your objectives for the next time you are calling on the customer
- Make a note of 'best practice' and the things that worked well as a reminder for other calls

The last couple of points may seem a little anal to some of you, however the planning process doesn't need to happen at a desk some time after nine o'clock at night or at the weekend.

By planning the next call while it's fresh in your mind means that in the weeks or months that pass between your next visit, the pre-call objectives are already in place.

YOU DECIDE Just a quick note to all those still worried about all this planning denting your style somehow.

If you walk into the call and an enormous opportunity that no one could have predicted knocks you over, just make a judgement call.

Ditch your existing plans if you need to, but be prepared enough to achieve something worthy of your time while you are there.

 OK, you are the customer again.

You are still *incredibly* busy, you still have all the problems, you have far too much to get done - just then an excited sales puppy bounds in. You smile and say; "So, what exciting opportunities have you got for me today, which of my many problems are you here to solve?"

And the representative says "I have nothing of any interest, I've just nipped in for a chat!"

Well I'd tell you to get lost – you might be paid for doing nothing, but I'm certainly not!

真 I have a friend who was promoted to National Account Manager, a huge jump as it was straight from field sales.

He had attended the account handovers with the incredibly well respected former NAM and realised that this national account lark wasn't all that difficult, everybody was very friendly.

A week or two later, he called one of his new customers while driving close by her office and asked if she was free for a last minute call.

She was.

He settled down, the secretary made them both a drink, and she asked him what it was that was so urgent for her to stop what she was doing. And he said,

"Nothing, I just fancied a coffee and a chat."

Needless to say he didn't finish his drink.

Setting Objectives

Let's split objectives into two camps;

- The objectives that are set for you by your business – **Company Objectives**
- **Call objectives** – objectives that you and your immediate line manager will set which help you achieve the company objectives.

Types of Objective

The company objectives should be fairly obvious to you; the business will announce them at sales meetings, annual sales conferences and through company-wide correspondence on a fairly regular basis

A call objective however is specific to one account; these are the objectives that you set before you go in to each call.

If your company objectives are clear you will have a firm idea of what you want to achieve in each account and they will subsequently fall into three further groups;

Remedial

This is where you call to correct a negative situation such as an unfortunate customer service incident or the outlet reneging on a current listing agreement.

Prospective

This type of objective is set with potential customers who you currently do not trade with or who do not currently list your entire portfolio. These can range from setting up a firm proposal meeting with the buyer to actually walking out with an order.

Improvement

With this kind of call objective you hope to build on your current relationship with extra listings or promotional activities.

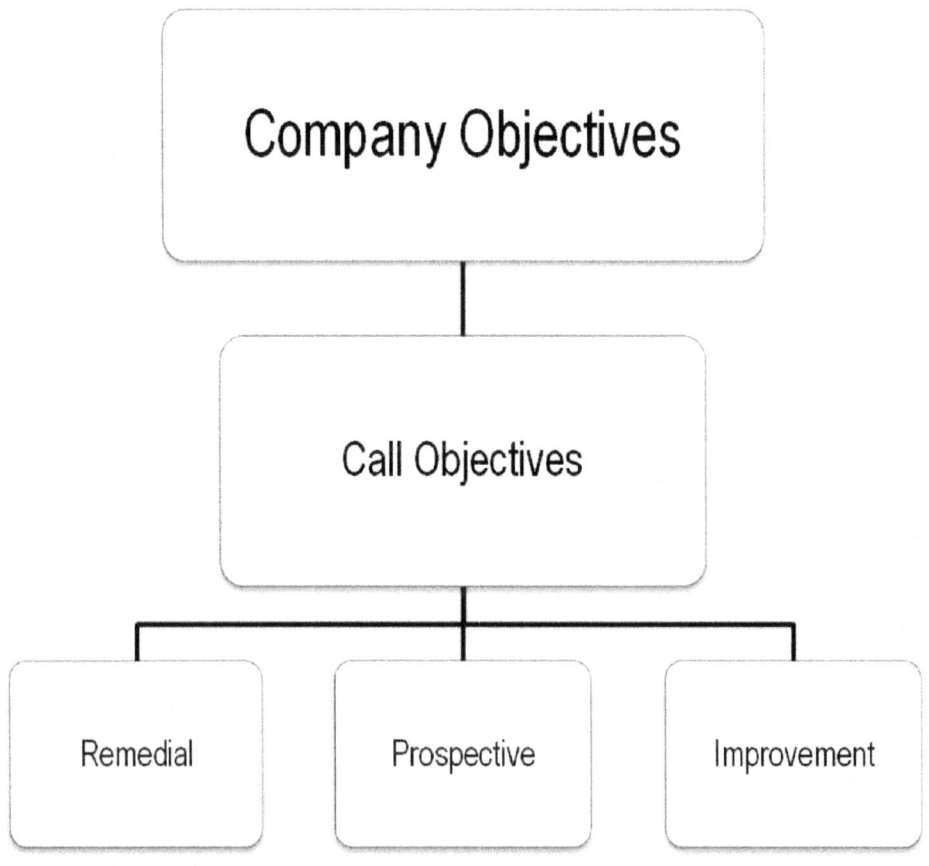

Figure 3 - Types of Objective

SMART Objective Setting

Many people talk about working **SMART** or having **SMART** objectives, like it's one of those secret acronyms that only those 'in the know' share amongst each other.

Well, just so you know, **SMART** stands for;

Figure 4 - Smart Objective Setting

The only reason for a business not to set SMART objectives is so that its sales team will never know if it has been successful, and no business would want to do that would it?

So, as an example, let's take a fairly generic objective and turn it into a SMART objective.

Your business says;

"Sell more of our Brands!"

And you think, "Well that isn't very specific is it, which brand? How will I know when I've sold as much as you want me to?"

So we introduce some SMART thinking.

Specific

"Sell more of **Brand H**."

Take that a little further so that we know when we have won.

Measurable and Achievable

Based on last year's figures "Sell 10% more of Brand H"

That's a little more understandable

Relevant

Based on last year's figures "Sell 10% more Brand H" **because as a business we are 9% behind our nearest competitor**.

Time Related

Based on last year's figures "Sell 10% more Brand H **between October and November**" because as a business we are 9% behind our nearest competitor.

SMART objectives should be set personally in line with company directives based on their own specific mix of;

- Sales Volume
- Distribution
- New Listings
- Pricing
- Profitability

But remember; whatever it is that you set out to achieve don't start focusing on something else.

For instance, if you are a sales manager and you have to improve sales by 20% don't reward your team or yourself for merchandising outlets; **reward them for selling 20% more**.

I use this quote in a lot of my courses and workshops;

> *"Happy, fulfilled, stretched but supported people generally achieve the most at work and get the most from life.*
>
> *They drain a lot of swamps – and have pretty good time doing it.*
>
> *However, many of us face a few alligators ….. those subversive obstacles that get in the way of a productive, high achieving but low stress kind of life.*
> *Some of them we make ourselves, some of them are placed there by other people. Some of them just are."*
>   – **Get Ahead; Give a Damn**

Simply put, if your objective is to drain the swamp, drain it.

Don't clear it of alligators or plant herbaceous borders or decorate it with garlands – those are just jobs that you'd rather do than the job at hand.

Set your objective and drain the swamp – keep focused and achieve what you set out to achieve.

3

Earn the Right

"The golden rule for every businessman is this; Put yourself in your customer's place!"
Orison Swett Marden

An important aspect of this part of the sales process is 'building rapport'.

Some sales trainers will talk about the 'Prime Opening Statements' and '30 second sales adverts' – but let's be frank – when you walk onto those premises for the first time, the last thing your customer wants to see is some thrusty young individual with his hand outstretched, spouting benefits out of context.

However you need to be confident enough in those first thirty seconds to keep the conversation going.

So, you need to be able to string together a paragraph that points out;
- Who you are
- Who you work for
- What they do
- What you do for your company

Then lead into a something interesting for their business (take a look at WIIFM later on) and finish with why now is a good time for them to be involved.

If you work with a wholesale business the response will probably be;

"If you can't beat my current price of Brand X then I'm not interested!"

However, if you work for a brand owner it may go something like;

"I'm happy with Brand X, but if you guys want to pay me a listing fee of £XXXXX or sponsor my pointless evening which does nothing but bolster my ego, I'll think about it."

The secret here is not to be phased by whatever it is that comes at you – clearly, what they are asking for is in the extreme, to either put you off or rip you off – go with it.

Don't agree to anything, don't sign anything, don't do anything – just ask them for some more details.

Then when you have started a conversation, you have started to build rapport.

There will have been many sales people before you got there who would have walked out with their tails between their legs; scared of the big, bad customer, **but we didn't walk in to walk straight out again did we?**

Sometimes they might just turn round and say;

"Look, I'm happy with what I've got, I'm really busy; I can't see you now."

If that's the case ask;

"When would it be a good time / day to come back?"

You see none of the above at any time said – *"You will never supply me!"*

They just need a bit of patience and tact – they do not need some green sales rep getting up their nose.

Remember though, if you don't sell something eventually we are all going out of business, there is a position somewhere between over-polite and nasty-pushy which you need to find, you must book that appointment or move forward with your objectives at some point.

Coffee Break Catch Up Number 1

Building rapport, presenting ourselves in a professional manner, approaching the sales situation and why customers decide to go with our recommendation are vital components to starting the entire process – it won't matter how many clever closing techniques you've learnt if you haven't laid this first foundation stone.

Here's a thought;

If you felt unwell, would you follow the medical advice from a scruffy, over familiar man at the train station who claimed to be a doctor?

For those of you who have children – would you just go out for the evening and trust your kid's safety to a complete stranger?

Of course you wouldn't – you need to be able to TRUST!

You're a customer - you know how sales people and service providers make you feel when they engage with you.

Understand that these prospective customers (these fellow human beings) want to be able to trust you. They would really love for someone to come along and answer their questions and take away their problems – but if you walk in looking like an unmade bed, have forgotten to bring all the supporting information and tools required and go straight for the sale – well, how would you feel?

Here are a few pointers

- Look in the mirror, would you buy from you?

- If someone asked you how your product or service helped, could you answer in a single sentence?

- Plan out where you are going today, this week, this month

- Understand the purpose of each and every call

- The journal you write your notes in, your pen, your presentation material, your lap top case – do they shriek "I'M PROFESSIONAL"?

- Charge everything that needs charging the night before

- Pick a winning, positive, helpful and friendly attitude

- You're a guest, act like one

- Listen to, and interact with, the conversation that THEY want to have with you

- From today, start to create a reputation that precedes you.

Outlet Check

There is much you can learn about a business by using your powers of observation.

Time mO I've seen too many sales people start a conversation twenty questions before they needed to, let me explain.

If it's your first time to a customer's premises the brand name of the company who owns the business will be somewhere in the small print on its marketing materials, other POS will convey current promotions, events and social connections so that you can work out a rough outline of their target market and current clientele.

There will be many indicators pointing out who their current suppliers are, while a number of other factors will point out how much support they currently receive from them.

If you know them or they get to like you enough , they may let you into their back office or stockroom, so with all that information already at hand why do so many people start off with questions that just leave the customer itching to get back to what they were doing before they came in?

Some (but not all) of the things to mentally check over before you start a conversation;

- If you are a brand owner, what is the distribution status within these outlets, and what should the display position be?

- Is pricing correct

- Are sales figures up to date and correct?

- Are they up on last year?

- Where are they against target?

- What factors are contributing to that position

- How is the competition doing?

- Are all promotions up and running and is all the POS where it should be?

Stuff to bring up during the conversation;

- What are stock levels like?

- Why are sales as they are? Can we help in any way?

Building Rapport

It is not the customers job to make you feel comfortable, but for you to make the customer comfortable with the sales situation as a whole.

Remember the assumptions from figure 1?

The customer knows that you are there to sell; you must **Earn the Right** to engage in a full conversation.

Once you have partly justified why you are there, find out why the customer is willing to talk to you, gain a sense of the customers business, their needs and their problems.

It isn't always necessary to jump straight into business, however all customers know when salespeople are leading up to the;

"So, listen, let me tell you why I'm here."

Don't be too false, if you don't want to start a conversation about your business ask the customer about theirs.

Attract the customers' attention; introduce a benefit or two with regards to your product or service which has already been mentioned as an issue; remember, we need to build up a relationship here.

If the customer has only good things to say about your competition, get on board, join in the conversation – don't contradict a happy customer – just find out what they are doing so well and find a way of doing it better.

Building rapport is an on-going process, it isn't something you do at the beginning of the sales process and then move on to the next step, keep in mind that you are there because they are allowing you to be there, and they are allowing you to be there because they think you might be able to help them somehow.

Coffee Break Catch Up Number 2

A couple of years ago, I was asked to set up a Business Development Team for a national children's charity, working with businesses of all shapes and sizes and essentially "selling in" what we did as a charity.

We recruited partners who would help us organise everything from a dress down Friday in their office to a full blown charity Christmas ball for their staff party.

I learnt a lot from that experience.

I learnt that my original, external view of the charity sector and the way the general public interacted with that world was way off the mark.

And I was reminded of an incredibly valuable sales lesson from one particular **CHUGGER**.

Chugger stands for Charity Mugger, they're the individuals who stand on the street and ask you to sign up to their good cause right there on the spot, and it's incredibly tough work.

I interviewed a chap for one of my business development roles on a stormy day in a Cornish hotel overlooking the sea.

I asked him, with regards to his recent apprenticeship as a chugger, what it was about *that* experience that was going to help him to become a successful Business Development Manager.

I have been repeating his answer ever since.

"When you're on the street you have 45 seconds to greet people politely, get their attention and then explain the problem, the solution and why they should act right now."

Fabulous!

Recently, I embarked on a project to help sales individuals and business owners with a series of 1 to 1 coaching sessions - and that simple sentence has proved to be the solution to a large proportion of their problems, fears and failures.

You see it sounds really simple – **problem, solution, action** – but that's what most sales people haven't really thought about.

So what can you learn from Chuggers?

Ask yourself these questions;

- Your product or service will ease a pain or deliver pleasure which one is it?

- How does it benefit them; what does it really do for your customer?

- So what problem are you solving?

Now in a sentence that takes less than 45 seconds to read aloud, explain;
- What the problem is (try starting off with a phrase like "Do you ever find that...")

- How your product or service solves it, work in some proof ("Your neighbour / competition discovered that..")

- Why they should act now (without making it sound like a threat or a cheesy "time is running out" line)

It's harder than it sounds – you have to turn your viewpoint to that of the customers, this isn't just about selling skills it's about understanding buying motives – an area which the charity sector really understands.

Which means that this isn't about what you're selling, it's about the effect it will have on your prospect – what it will do for them, how it will make them feel and how they will be perceived by their peers afterwards.

Understand that and you can start helping people instead of simply selling to them.

5 other helpful things we can learn from chuggers

- Smile a natural smile – no one ever kicked a dog wagging its tail

- You can dress like an unwashed, new age free spirit if you want to; just as long as you don't mind everyone crossing the street to completely avoid you.

- The general public know you have something to sell, cut out the false sounding and meaningless small talk and get to the point

- Believe in yourself, if you start acting like a scared, nervy little baby bird you will make me feel really, really uncomfortable.

- Push me too hard and I'll make my excuses and leave, treat me right and identify with how I feel about this problem and I'll hear you out.

Deep Listening

Now is a good time to discuss the art of deep listening.

The best way to describe this is with the Chinese symbol for the verb "to listen".

Essentially it reads "I give you my ears, my eyes, my undivided attention and my heart" which is just about the best definition for listening I've ever heard.

Most sales people ask questions for the sake of asking questions – they rarely hear the answers. Others never stop talking long enough to warrant a response.

When we come to our next section we will discuss how to ask appropriate questions, but it's all a bit pointless if you haven't listened.

Figure 5 - The Chinese Pictogram "To Listen"

Listening is all about being there at that moment in time.
It isn't checking your watch because you have three more calls to do, nor is it staring around at the clientele while the customer is talking.

It is about showing respect and taking an interest.

The customer has given up their time to see you, this is the first step to a successful sale, don't blow it because your attention span doesn't stretch far enough!

Here are some essential rules to deep listening;

- First of all, listen to fully understand and then respond – and only in that order. If you didn't understand say so and ask again.

- Do not spend the time that a customer is responding to your question, or trying to tell you something, thinking of your next question.

- If you have already made up your mind of what the answer is going to be, why ask? Alternatively, ask, listen and learn.

- There will be a point when you become conscious that you stopped listening, turn it back on again. If you think you missed something important, politely cover it off again

- Don't interrupt

- Keep eye contact as much as you can (without being spooky) and react accordingly with appropriate listening sounds and facial reactions.

- Qualify what you have heard e.g. "So if I heard you right, you are saying that…"

- Remember your manners

- You are not always right

- Make notes or put your hands down – don't fidget.

4

Ask the Appropriate Questions

"He who asks a question may be a fool for five minutes, but he who never asks a question remains a fool forever." **Chinese Proverb**

Being able to understand a situation well enough to present a solution needs a particular set of questioning skills and now that we understand the equally important ability to listen to the answers, here is how we do it.

Questioning Techniques

In the first chapter we mentioned the customer who walks into a DIY store to buy a drill, he doesn't really want a drill – he wants a hole!

A bad salesperson will present the drills that are on offer, a good salesperson will discuss the desired hole with the customer.

The ability to ask questions enables us to ask about that hole and supply the appropriate drill.

What we are looking to do with these techniques is;

- Establish the customers' needs
- Make sure they feel part of the buying decision
- To collect information
- To qualify and confirm their genuine interest
- To keep some element of control during the meeting

Types of Questions

The two most talked about questioning techniques are **'OPEN PROBES'** and **'CLOSED PROBES'**.

Open Probes

The clue is in the title really, they are used to 'OPEN UP' the conversation.
If you ask an Open Probe the customer shouldn't be able to just answer with a YES or a NO and they often start with the words;

Who; What; Where; When; Why; How; Which

Figure 6 - Open Probes

So, as an example, instead of asking "Is tonight your busiest night?" you ask "When is your busiest night?"

Closed Probes

Closed Probes are the complete opposite; you use them when you want to bring the conversation to a shuddering halt.

"So, if I can do all that for you do we have a deal?"

But the shape of the conversation shouldn't just look like a funnel, steadily decreasing towards the final closing question.

It should ebb and flow in waves.

Using open probes to gain information – to open up the shape of the conversation - and then closed probes to clarify your understanding – leaving only the opportunity for a yes or no.

Occasionally you might wish to lead your customer into a particular direction or to qualify something they have just said these are called Leading Probes.

Leading Probes

Leading Probes control a situation in a way that qualifies what the customer has just said and gets you back on track, for instance;

"So you are saying that you have too many old brands in stock and you need to work out which you will be replacing is that correct?

"You said you thought that was a good idea before, how do you think you'll be moving forward?"

Misconceptions about Questioning Techniques

Some people seem to think that OPEN questions are good and CLOSED questions are bad.

That isn't the case at all. They are just useful tools with their own place and purpose.

It is their selection and how they are used which is either good or bad – you wouldn't use a screwdriver to bang in a nail would you?

Using any tool inappropriately will cause you problems.

An over use of any type of question, open or closed, will present difficulties.

If all you have are questions, questions, questions - the following problems will occur:

Your customer will switch off

There is a limit to the number of questions a customer can put up with. If you are going to ask a series of questions one after the other, the likelihood is that their responses will just get shorter and shorter as the interrogation continues.

Your customer will become defensive

They know you are trying to sell something to them, they are already quite cautious, but if you just go in with question after question you will starve them of their 'psychological oxygen' and the conversation will just dry up.

They are being careful with their choice of words in case you trap them with your magical and mysterious salesperson ways. If you question them into a corner they will just refuse to continue.

Remember - Asking Questions isn't the Objective.

You are trying to sell something in or increase business somehow, questions won't get the order by themselves, a couple of answers would really help too.

I'm sure you have heard this before, but I'll repeat it because it's undoubtedly true;

You've got two ears and one mouth and they should be used in that ratio.

So how do we use these techniques without scaring the life out of the customer?

We use them to **Solve the Problem**

Coffee Break Catch Up Number 3

Here's a thing – there isn't a customer on earth who wants to listen to your sales presentation if they don't believe they have any reason to; so how is it that more businesses and sales people practise presentation skills than questioning techniques?

As I've mentioned before, one my favourite little bits of wisdom is this:

"When a customer walks into a DIY store to buy a drill, they don't want a drill, they want a hole! Good sales people discover exactly what kind of hole the customer needs, the bad ones just talk about drills."

I heard this version recently and it made me smile;

"Sales people always want to talk about the scratch, but rarely ask about the itch!"

While you're asking your questions, you must distinguish between statements that indicate your prospect is currently dissatisfied (called Implied Needs) and statements which show a real desire to find a solution (Explicit Needs).

Implied Needs do not necessarily mean a prospect is ready to change, whereas Explicit Needs are usually key indicators of wanting to make a difference.

A few years ago I was introduced to a technique known as **PURE** questioning;

Probe – Question to determine the current situation
Uncover – Use questions which uncover an Implied Need
Recognise – Develop the problem through further questions so the customer recognises an Explicit Need
Evaluate – Ask questions to confirm that the need really exists and which enable you to build value into your recommendations.

It works like this;

- Use open probes - which the customer cannot simply answer yes or no to, to open up the conversation. They usually start with the words Who, What, Where, When, Why and How.

- Use closed probes to close the conversation right down, when you need a definitive yes or no

- Probe to find out exactly what is making your prospect itch

- Next, ask questions to determine how annoying that itch really is and what's really causing it

- Now probe to discover the benefits and value a solution would deliver to the customer

5

Solve the Problem

"It is one of the beautiful compensations of life that no man can sincerely try to help another without helping himself." **Ralph Waldo Emerson**

When we fully understand the situation, when we know what it is that we have within our toolbox which will deliver a benefit to the customer we present it professionally and effectively.

Our questions are directed at delivering value to the customer rather than just becoming a cost.

For instance;

The customer is experiencing frequent problems with their current supplier's deliveries.

Now don't just jump in and tell them how wonderful your business is, start probing a little deeper.

"Sounds like those deliveries are causing you some grief, what are the knock-on effects?"

You see, instead of being so eager to sell you can become consultative with your approach, you discuss their business, their problems.

Here's another one;

The quality of the Product H in his catalogue is inconsistent, but he doesn't want the hassle of changing his list or his supplier.

"But how much hassle is the inconsistency issue – didn't you say that it reflects badly on your good name in the customers eyes?"

Once you feel you are ready to present your solution you will need to differentiate between something called FEATURES, ADVNTAGES AND BENEFITS.

Features, Advantages and Benefits

Features, advantages and benefits are as relevant to an account manager in charge of supplying the biggest multiple accounts in the country as they are to a new representative selling their first box to a single outlet.

However, sales people always seem to talk about the features of their product or service.

A few quick definitions;

Features – What it is

Statements describing some characteristic of a product or service

Advantages – What it does

Statements showing how a product or product feature can be used to help the buyer

Benefits – What it will do for the buyer

Statements showing how the product, product feature or advantage meets and Explicit Need addressed by the buyer

Implied Need

A statement by the buyer regarding problems, difficulties or dissatisfactions with the existing situation

Explicit Need

A clear, unambiguous statement of the buyers' wants, desires or intentions.

Customers only buy what these features will do for them – and these are called benefits.

The trick is to uncover the customer's needs and match these with the benefits of your offering.

Remember the customer in the DIY store buying a drill, he doesn't really want a drill – he wants a hole!

A bad salesperson will present the drills that are on offer, talk about what they are made of, where they come from, which brand did well in tests – those are all features

The good salesperson discusses the hole, finds out what the customer really wants and aligns that with what is on offer.

Your products deliver benefits and solve problems for customers; do you know what they are?

The question you must be able to answer is this:

How can you turn the features of your product or service into the benefits most relevant to your customer?

WII FM

No, it's not a radio station, it stands for;

What's In It For Me!

That is what your customers want to know.

They don't care what size the bottle is, or the case configuration.

They are only listening to you explain the production techniques and country of origin because they have a slight personal interest in the subject and they feel that it is something they really should know.

What they want to know is what your bag of beans will do for them.

So, What Are Features?

Let's take a fruit based soft drink as an example;

Case size	24 x 275 ml
Individual bottle size	275 ml
Pallet Configuration	78 cases (24 x 275ml)
Flavours	Orange, Lemon, Blackcurrant, Cranberry

All those are features.

They may be important details, but they just don't help anyone out of context.

Other examples of features include;

- Taste
- Production process
- Packaging
- Ease of opening
- Position in market
- Market growth
- Quality
- Heritage
- International origin.

Your presentations will be peppered with them, they are everything that makes your product or service what it is – but, as your customer, they have no impact on my life or lifestyle until you show me how they **BENEFIT** me.

So, What Are Benefits?

A benefit is all about the customer.

It tells them "What's in it for me?" and "What does it do for me?"

It is the positive thing that is going to happen if they embark on a certain course or take a specific action.

Examples of Benefits

"There's no way your customers will miss this new POS; so far, everywhere that it has gone up, sales have gone through the roof"

"By offering a premium quality range of malt whiskies around Fathers Day - last year, new stockists witnessed an uptake in cash profit of 22%"

You see your customer is really only interested in what you have to offer if it:

- Increases sales
- Brings in more customers
- Somehow saves time or improves productivity
- Creates more profit
- Reduces costs
- Makes them look fabulous
- Makes them feel fabulous

So, now we have got that out of the way, it's time to present your solution.

Coffee Break Catch Up Number 4

The Story of the Magic Beans

The expert had sold the miracle cure to the customer – both were excited about it – the expert counted the money; packed everything back in the briefcase; shook hands and left.

The customer ran into the larger room.

"Look what I've got – this is amazing – just take a look at this!"

His friends, family, colleagues and customers gather round, staring with eager anticipation into the outstretched palm and say in unison,

"What on earth have you just bought?"

"These, my friends, are my magical beans!"

"Yeah Right!" the now worried group is concerned that one of their own has been fooled and hoodwinked by a travelling charlatan.

"Hold on, look what they do!" he cries.

However, the 3 "Magic Beans" do nothing.

How could this be, only thirty minutes ago he had been guaranteed miraculous results, the answer to all his prayers, there had been testimonials, proof that another young man, just like him, overcoming adversity with these simple beans.

The angry mob chase after the con artist, throw the beans in his face, take back the money, rip up the contract and leave him bruised wondering how it all went wrong.

OK, Change the magic beans for your product or service.

The customer has shown a clear interest in moving forward, what could go wrong?

You've left the proposal, samples and presentation materials –they just want to talk it over with their partner, discuss it with the staff in the back, show it to those who will use it most – get a better idea from the people at the frontline.

But your job is not to sell a magic trick that only works in your presence, because without you there to make the inanimate animate they will just foolishly hold out a few magic beans.

5 tips to avoid the Magic Bean scenario;

- When possible, present to ALL the decision makers

- Be prepared for, encourage, and then inoculate the most common objections.

- Be 100% honest with expected outcomes

- Realise that hardly any solution works completely by itself – educate the customer on the effort required to gain the required result

- Make sure what you've promised happens – even if you have to plant the beans yourself

6

Execute the Solution

"What you do today is important because you are exchanging a day of your life for it."
Anonymous

The Presentation

Topics to cover during your presentation will include;

- The Market in which the product or service operates and how it performs
- Details of the actual product or service
- Support that the customer can expect to help drive and create demand
- Profit expectations

A quick check list, make sure it also answers the following questions;

- ✓ What is it and why should the customer be interested?
- ✓ What is so different or special about what you have to offer?
- ✓ How does the customer benefit – how do we answer the customers question – "What's In It For Me?"

"If you can't explain it simply, you don't understand it well enough."
– **Albert Einstein**

Sales Presenter

Whatever format your sales presenter may take, make sure it's customer friendly – remember, it is for their benefit not yours.

For example; if you have had A4 presentation cards created, make sure that the writing, facts and figures are just short bullet points – readable from a distance, and vague enough to be simple talking points.

**If you can't just point at it with your pen, as a single fact,
then it has been expressed in a format which is too long for this purpose – this is not a letter – it is a presentation aid.**

You really should know the contents already; there is no need for you to read it. Hold it facing the buyer – not half way round, so that the customer can see the contents easily.

Without looking like you are selling an insurance policy, use your pen to highlight points and hold their attention, it is important to remember that the customer will always be able to read faster than you can speak, so don't let them get ahead of you

Also don't read it word for word, expand on the bullet points and try to associate each detail, fact or benefit with the customers business (without sounding patronising).

When you have finished with it, put it away or put it to one side so that there are no distractions.

If you are leaving it with the customer, let them read it, touch it, and ask questions about it before you move on. There is no point trying to move forward with the process until they are happy with what they have just heard and flushed the desire to examine it fully out of their system.

Samples

Don't assume that your customer has any level of awareness with regards to your range, always keep a small amount of samples with you where possible and keep them in first class condition.

真 Always make sure that you are using samples effectively.

There was a sales team which launched an RTD (Ready to Drink) product in the nineties, with the instruction from their Sales Director to make sure all the Senior Buyers tasted the product.

The trouble was, none of the Senior Buyers were anywhere near the target market, and they hated it. In fact most of them were fairly sold on the opportunity until they were coerced into trying it.

POS

If you have any corresponding POS material, now is the time for it to make an impact.

Once you have solved the problem, you put that solution into action.

That means knowing how to ask for the sale (or close), follow through with the required administration and keeping all your promises to the customer.

It is up to you to make sure everything that should happen does happen. Don't blame other departments, others will let you down – fact, as a department we cannot let our customers down.

Closing

The two biggest sales based "FEARS" that I come across more than any other, are the fear of PRICE and the fear of CLOSING.

Remember; you are there to sell, the customer knows that you are there to sell – the customer is expecting you to ask for the business sooner or later.

Time mO I have known people talk themselves out of a sale.
They missed the opportune moment, kept on going because they were afraid to ask, just after that the customer got bored and said goodbye.

When you get the buying signals – CLOSE THE DEAL!

Now I can understand that some sales people get nervous about closing because, on occasions, it can be the first point of the sales call where the buyer can say no.

But if you don't ask you're going to miss out on all those YES's!

Time mO From the moment a salesperson meets a Buyer, everything which is said or done is part of and is leading up to the Close.

In truth you should try to close as early as possible, that doesn't mean rushing through the first three parts of the sales process, it just means that once you have the sale in the bag – CLOSE IT!

But remember, when you've asked the question– SHUT UP.

> *"Often we are so eager to sell; we don't give the prospect enough room to buy."*
> — **Jeffrey Gitomer**

Buying Signals

You don't just have to 'feel' if the time is right, the customer will let you know that they are ready to move forward.

They might show some level of interest in your advertising campaign or how successful the product has been elsewhere, they aren't just being polite – they're interested.

If you hear any of these it is time to formulate a close;

"How soon could I have it?"
"Is it available now?"
"How much is it?"
"What else does your company do?"

Also, they might pose an objection – this may appear negative, but in reality they are asking whether it is right for them or not.

If the objection is presented to you as a question, they want to know more, once again they aren't just being polite, they have better ways to waste their lives than humouring you – they're interested.

They might actually say they want whatever it is you're there to present.

I have also watched too many salespeople completely ignore the phrase "Go on then, I'll give it a try!"

Types of Close

It is easy to think of these techniques as something from the dark ages of sales, or the kind of thing a street hustler would use on unsuspecting tourists, but ignore the silly names and read deeper into how they could help you ask for more business, and enable you to **help** your customers more often with the benefits your products and services have to offer.

Summary

Summarise the benefits briefly before actually closing.

Alternative

With this close, its impact is all down to the way you phrase the words. What you are trying to do is offer two alternatives that are both in your favour.

For example; *"78 or 156 cases – which do you think?"*

Concession

Essentially starting high so you can be knocked down to the amount you want to achieve, gracefully reducing the amount, so that the customer has had some influence over the order process.

"So we can let you have the promotional materials for an order of twenty cases?"

"I can't take twenty"

"Really, What do you believe is reasonable then? I can probably sneak it through for fifteen for you."

Assumptive

You finish off your presentation with the assumption that the customer is ready to move forward.

"So, in view of our conversation earlier I'll send in two cases of each"

Shelf Space

Similar to the assumptive, but with this close you start to discuss how much space the customer will give to the new listing when it comes in.

Future Benefit

Used, for example, before an imminent price rise or tax increase.

"If you order today, the order will be delivered at pre-budget pricing"

Link / Agreement Statement

Build agreement on a chain of smaller points before introducing the important one.

Fear of Loss

If the customer doesn't act now, you won't be able to offer the deal.

"I've only been given a small allocation for this promotion, when I come back next week they'll all be gone."

Handling Objections

It may not be easy to view a customer disagreeing with you or appearing to be awkward as an opportunity but actually their objection is taking you closer to the close.

If handled correctly, objections tell you what the customer wants to buy and therefore, what you need to sell to them.

The customer isn't trying to pick a fight, they are simply trying to work out if they are actually interested or not.

If a customer is asking questions or seeing potential problems, then they must be imagining themselves with your product or service – that's positive

If a customer raises an objection you should;

Listen

Remember the rules regarding deep listening techniques. Be attentive to the customers' viewpoint and do not interrupt. If you interrupt you are basically saying that you don't value their opinion.

Ask questions

Clarify your understanding of the objection

Verify and restate

Let the customer know you have listened by restating the issue raised.

For example;

"I can see why you might think................However......"

Respect their point of view

You don't have to agree, but you must not ignore it or ridicule it.

Does it really matter?

Check that the issue is a real issue with some speculative questions.

"If that wasn't an issue would you place an order?"

"I'll see what I can do about that, if I can sort it out, can we proceed?"

There are times when a customer is just trying to be awkward, but if you really have a sincere objection, determine if it is based on fact or misunderstanding.

> *"He who is afraid to ask is ashamed of learning."*
> — **Danish Proverb**

Objections Justified or Unjustified?

If the objection is based on fact, we call this a **justified objection**.

If the objection is based on a misunderstanding, then it is an **unjustified objection**.

Handling Justified Objections

If the objection is justified, then the customer has raised an objection which is a real obstacle to making the sale.

To countermand this, put the problem into perspective or show how the benefits outweigh the obstacle.

Handling Unjustified Objections

Usually, this is based on a misunderstanding caused by lack of information / incorrect information.

If this is the case, it is not the customers fault – the sales person must take responsibility if a customer doesn't understand the product, service or benefits.

Anticipating Objections

If possible try to anticipate any objections that may arise.

Virtually all objections can be anticipated.

You will find that the same old objections will be raised time after time for a particular product or proposal; honestly, customers aren't gathering in secret groups trying to invent new problems for you!

If you can make sure that you have prepared responses to these and have practised delivering them in a confident manner, you will be able to move the sale forward.

Sometimes you will come across what we call "special situation" objections.

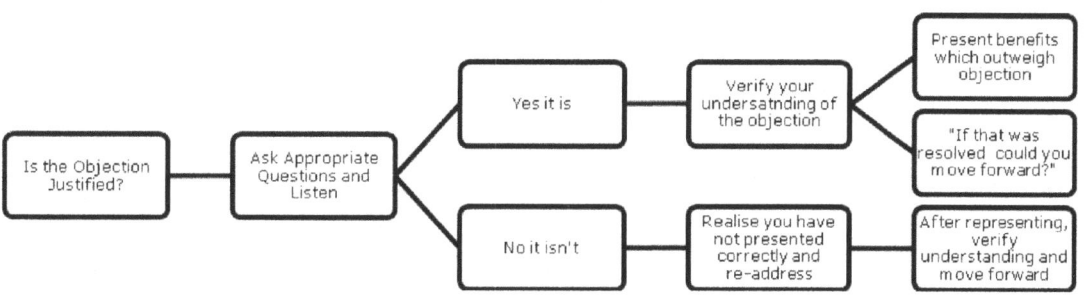

Figure 6 - Handling Objections

Special Situation Objections

One day you won't know the answer – it's bound to happen eventually!

When this happens, admit it – do not pretend to know or fake an answer.

Customers appreciate honesty and can smell "sales gibberish" ten miles away.

If you do not heed this advice and are found out, you will run the risk of being seen as an untrustworthy joke – and when you look back on it in years to come, you will shudder with embarrassment – trust me.

I once heard a retail salesperson, in a high street wine merchant store tell a customer that there was no difference between Champagne and Apple Cider.

However new or naive he was, that was just foolish. The customer probably knew that wasn't true, and avoided him on every subsequent visit.

Bluffing your way round an objection maybe just as foolish for you if your customer knows a little more than they are letting on!

Objections in disguise

The objection raised may be masking another, much more basic problem.

The only way to get to the heart of this issue is to question and verify until you uncover the real issue.

For instance, maybe it isn't that they do not wish to stock the new line at all, maybe;

- They have no further credit with their supplier
- They have an existing (confidential) contract or agreement in place, that would be broken if they took yours
- They didn't like your predecessor

I could carry on with a whole list of potentials, but you get the idea.

Just the wrong product and customer mix

Nobody has a 'one size fits all' product or service that works with everyone.

Remember go and fish where the fish are, and don't get too upset about it – you can't save them all!

真 A friend of mine went for an interview once and was asked to sell the interviewers a pen.

This is an old technique, and the scene maybe familiar to you if you have ever been to get a job in a tough sales environment.

They want to see you in action, see how you handle objections, what are you like with features and benefits.

For the record I think it's a nonsense – how does the sales person know the provenance of the pen, its worth, cost or value?

So my friend went straight in *"Do you want to buy a pen?"*

To which his interviewer answered *"No!"*

"OK then, there are lots of people out there who need pens – I'm sorry I wasted your time."

And he left.

A moment later he popped his smiling face back round the door.

He didn't get the job, but what he does understand is that you can't win every battle, sometimes there are more productive and profitable uses for your time than arguing the toss with someone who is never going to see your point or get the obvious benefits to their business.

Go and pick the low hanging fruit first.

Surround the difficult customers business with success stories from competitors – if it really is a benefit and tremendous opportunity they mostly come round.

Some just don't – go figure!

Here are a few reminders and tips for handling objections

Take your time

Think about the situation, the problem at hand.
Take deep breaths - there is no need to react immediately.

Keep your temper

Telling customers that they have ugly children isn't going to win the deal, stay calm!

Become a detective

Study the clues, analyse;

- Is it a real objection?
- Was it just a question?
- What does it reflect?
- Disinterest?
- Misunderstanding?
- Do you fully understand it?

Clarify the objection

Call it by its real name

Verify your understanding of the situation

Explain the situation to the satisfaction of the customer without sounding like you agree with them.

Handle it

Address the issue, offer a solution, point out the misunderstanding (without being patronising), and agree a middle ground.

Always worth asking *"Is this really necessary to move forward?"*

As an example;

"Does this car come in British racing green?"
"Is that the only colour you are interested in?"
"No, I was just wondering!"
"Well I'm afraid we don't, but let's have a look at the colours we do have shall we, I'm sure we have another that will turn out to be the right one for you!"

Fear of Price

真 When I was about eight years old there was a sign in the corner shop window for tennis balls. Suddenly overwhelmed with an urge to buy one, I rushed home and asked my mother if I could have the money. To my surprise she said, *"Yes, OK, how much do you need?"*

Flushed with a sense of embarrassment which I still can't explain, I knocked the price down by about 30%. I don't know why, maybe I only like delivering good news, maybe I didn't think she'd give me the full amount – either way I got less than I actually needed, making the whole process a little pointless.

When, I got back to the store, the only thing I could afford was a ping pong ball, which I bought (so that the trip hadn't been a complete waste of time!?!), and then hid it from my mother because I felt stupid.

I'm telling you this because it came rushing (embarrassingly) back to me last week when I overheard a negotiation, and the salesman got me thinking – *"how many grown-ups are doing something similar with their company's money?"*

Price really embarrasses some people. When a sales person has some flexibility with margin to "get the business" there are times when their inner voice just wants to knock a little off, that the amount could possibly be a little on the high side and anyway, the margin flexibility was probably built in for a moment just like this.

真 Let me tell you another story;

Skip ahead about ten years from the tennis ball debacle and I'm working for a business that imports the most expensive, stylish and technologically cutting edge aquariums around at that time.

If you wanted one of these, you took your home aquarium hobby really seriously - or could afford someone else to look after it for you.

So, one day this guy calls and asks if we have a certain model in stock, I take the call, check the storeroom and call him back.

"Yes we do! It costs £1,000. You want to pick it up this afternoon? OK, see you then."

So the guy turned up, introduced himself and he inspected the aquarium.

He turned to the most senior salesman in the room and asked *"How much discount for cash?"*

To which Mr. Senior Salesman replies *"10%"*

So the customer pulled £1,000 in cash out of his wallet, counted £100 from the top and gave us the £900.

Now as a business there was no 10% discount rule, there was flexibility sure, but there was nothing in the induction about cash discounts.

Let's have a look at that again;

The customer had clearly come equipped to buy the aquarium; he had called to check the price, travelled to pick it up himself and brought the full amount in cash.

So why did the salesman feel the need to give him a discount?

Maybe he only liked to deliver 'good' news, maybe he didn't think the customer would give him the full amount – either way he got less than he actually could have got, 10% less – could you imagine increasing your turnover by 10%?

I'll tell you something, it's a lot harder than decreasing your turnover by 10%!

Since then, I have come to learn that the price of a product should always be the amount that it is worth to the customer, so ask yourself this;

Are you ever embarrassed when you tell people how much they will have to pay for your product or service?

Why?

If you are ripping people off, then quite right, feel embarrassed, get out while you can and find a product which you can feel proud of.

But if it's worth it, if the price is fair, what's your problem?

Here's another question;

Those shoes you wear to work, were they the cheapest on the high street?

I bet they weren't. Someone out there was selling cheaper shoes than you bought; so why did you buy them?

Was it because you wanted them, liked the colour, liked the style, made you feel good about yourself, because they were a really nice fit, was the sales person pleasant?

 Try this exercise;

Write down the price of your service or product next to the price of three competitor prices.

Then, underneath the prices that are less expensive than yours, write three good reasons why your product or service is a better buy.

Similarly, for all those that are more expensive, find three things that both your product and theirs have in common.

Those are the reasons that make what you have to offer special and value for money, they should form a major part of your defence during objections regarding price.

Simply put, these few sentences should enable you to prove why your product or service costs as much as it does.

7

Administration & Post Call Evaluation

"The key is not to prioritise what's on your schedule, but to schedule your priorities."
Stephen R Covey

Ah, if there is one word to strike a chill into most salespeople it is ADMINISTRATION.

For some reason, every Monday morning the entire internet goes down and 60% of weekly reports can't be delivered by their deadline, no other day of the week – just Monday.

There are usually three objectives attached to routine administration;

- ➢ To communicate information to your business and hierarchy
- ➢ To measure and monitor your performance
- ➢ To maintain reliable records

Administration is incredibly important to the sales process; however, as most sales people are action and creation orientated, the process can often seem like a waste of valuable time.

Sales Figures

As sales people we sell stuff, count how much we sold and the profit we made when we sold it, and hold that up against are objectives.

You need up-to-date figures; you need accurate past figures to compare with.

You need to have a system that tracks your progress with prospects, current customers, dead accounts, sleeping giants and wasters.

Customer Records

There is an old, well worn phrase that escapes the lips of tired, overworked and ignored sales managers;

"Keep your records up to date, what happens if you get hit by a bus tomorrow – how will the next guy know what was going on?"

And what every salesperson thinks is this;

"I won't give a monkeys backside about it - I'll be the one who was hit by a bus!"

I find it quite laughable that we use that phrase so often, surely the salespersons motivation is no different from the customers, they will always ask.

What's In It For Me!

So here, I am asking that as a sales professional - on this occasion - you think of no-one but yourself.

Keep your records up to date so they are useful for **YOU** and write your sales reports so that **YOU** can gain some use from them in months to come.

If you get hit by a bus and they are then useful to someone else – great – but make sure that they are the most useful to you.

For each and every call you make, do you always have the following pieces of information?

- Outlet contacts, address, outlet specific information
- Outlet objectives
- Recent sales information

An old Sales Director of mine came out on some calls with me at the beginning of my career and asked for an agenda for the next call – I didn't have one.

He took me through the advantages of having my objectives written down and the further advantages of having a copy to leave with the customer.

We discussed having clear objectives earlier, but to have them clearly spaced on a page which can be used to make special extra notes under specific headings is great for referring to later, especially if you have to create any further correspondence.

To be able to leave a copy with the customer detailing information regarding pricing, delivery dates, promotional activity or pending increases (even if it has to be changed by hand) gives them something physical, some proof of the conversation, before the official confirmation arrives.

When making notes I look to use something we used to call the branch system, rediscovered over recent years as **Mind Mapping**.

It enables me to scribble ideas and conversations down quickly while connecting them to set agenda points.

Should the conversation move away from my objectives, if customers start to contradict themselves or there are inconsistencies throughout the conversation, I can spot them easily so that they don't distract from what I am trying to achieve.

Evaluation

> *"Insanity: doing the same thing over and over again and expecting different results"*
>
> **Albert Einstein**

So, you walk out of call and on to the next one, but did you do everything you wanted to do?

Were all objectives achieved?

- Yes
    - What should we be proud of?
    - What can we use in other accounts?

- No
    - Why? What went wrong?
    - How can we put it right?
    - Was the objective SMART

What did we do well or badly?

Was there anything else we could have done?

What should the next call objectives be for this account?

Notes

Notes

Notes

About Chris Murray

Chris Murray has become prominent as an inspirational speaker, author and sales training coach by delivering a down to earth, high energy message which shows sales teams, managers and directors how to become more efficient, more productive and as a result more successful and happier in what they do.

His career saw him rise through the ranks from Field Sales to Sales Director, and with more than twenty years experience working with companies which have included LVMH, SOPEXA, Herman Miller, Minolta and Jim Beam Brands, Chris has presented programmes to sales teams and managers whose portfolios have encompassed everything from water to Champagne.

Today Chris conducts more than 100 seminars, speeches and workshops a year for a huge variety of companies and organisations in Britain and overseas.

His workshops and keynote speeches challenge teams to re-examine what it means to be "in sales" and requires them to stand back and view the whole experience from a refreshingly different angle.

His range of topics includes:

- Field Sales

- Key and National Account Management

- Sales Management

- Mission, Vision and Values

Chris is founder and Managing Director of Varda Kreuz Training, one of the UK's most innovative training and development organisations

For more information about Chris, you can call him direct on +44 (0) 161 935 8183 or email info@vardakreuztraining.com

About Varda Kreuz Training

Mission Statement

To help sales teams become more effective, more productive and as a result more successful and happier at what they do.

Varda Kreuz Training is one of the UK's most innovative training and development organisations, specialising in tailored and bespoke programmes which offer a wide range of business solutions.

The team at Varda Kreuz Training have many years experience, specialising in key business development training spanning various industry sectors.

Our ethos is based on enabling clients to access skills deliberately, aid in the discovery of existing problems and culminates in the ability to equip clients with tools to achieve the solution.

Once we know what you want to achieve, when we fully understand your requirements, we will present our recommendations.

Your business and team are unique, that means that your training and development should be too.

Programmes and Services

- The Selling With EASE workshops
- The REAL Account Management workshops
- Sales Managers Guide to Achieving FAME workshops
- TIGER Networking workshops
- Achieving the END Result workshops

To find out more information contact us by emailing info@vardakreuztraining.com or call +44 (0)161 935 8183 to book a free no obligation consultation

**We are not a giant, faceless corporate training company delivering generic, uninspiring, workaday courses.
We are VARDA KREUZ**

Lightning Source UK Ltd.
Milton Keynes UK
UKOW04f0555300117

293174UK00010B/370/P

9 781849 140799